LEAN LOCK

The Groundbreaking New Method for Making More Putts

Brian Tennyson

COPYRIGHT © BRIAN TENNYSON 2021

Published by BRIAN TENNYSON PROMOTIONS LLC
First Edition

LIBRARY OF CONGRESS CATALOGING-IN-PUBLICATION DATA
has been applied for

ISBN 978-1-7368887-0-4

All photos courtesy of Brian J. Tennyson

Printed in the United States of America

CONTENTS

PREFACE

By Brian Tennyson

If you are reading this book, it is safe to assume you are either simply curious or have struggled with your putting. Putting is critically important to scoring and to our enjoyment of the game since it accounts for up to about 30-50% of our score on any given day. If your long game is good but you putt poorly, you feel like you have wasted a good ball-striking round. If your long game is weak but you sink a lot of putts, you are happy because you feel like you have maximized the potential score. Golf is simply a lot more fun when we are striking pure putts and making more of them.

My personal journey with golf started at seven years old hitting whiffle balls into soup cans buried in our backyard with my older brother Roger. My only club was a sawed-off 4-iron with masking tape as the grip. By the age of 10, I could break 40 occasionally for 9-holes and by age 14, I was shooting in the 60s for 18-holes. Eventually I became a top junior, amateur and collegiate golfer, winning eight NCAA individual titles before qualifying for the PGA Tour at the age of 24. On the PGA Tour I was a runner-up twice and won two international titles. I finished 29th on the PGA Tour money list in 1990, played in multiple U.S. Opens, U.S. PGA Championships and The Masters.

After reading the previous paragraph, you may be thinking I must have always been a great putter. The truth is that my putting has fluctuated from utterly fantastic to miserably horrible throughout my golfing life. Even though I played professional golf at the highest level, I struggled to truly understand how to consistently putt well. In search of consistency, I tried virtually every instruction theory and putting method that exists, which ultimately only confused me more. I would find a method that worked well for a while, even for long stretches if I practiced for an hour or two every day, but eventually my putting would go south again. For most of my life I was confused and uncertain about how to strike pure putts. Should I control the stroke with my big muscles, feel it in my fingers, forward press, let my arms hang, keep my upper arms against my torso, point my elbows out, tuck them against my body, lead the stroke with my left hand, hit with my right hand, grip the club more in my fingers, grip it in my palms/lifeline, use an arc stroke, use a pendulum stroke, use a straight-back-straight-through stroke, etc.? Please, make it stop!

At the height of my confusion, I asked myself a simple question: "What needs to happen to strike a pure putt and what factors could I control to make that happen consistently?" My pursuit of answering that simple question eventually led me to the firm understanding that, no matter how you accomplish it, **in order to strike a pure putt, at the moment of impact, the putter must be traveling at an ascending angle as close to straight along the intended start line as possible with the club face square to that line.** With that as my guiding principle, I cast aside all conventional theories and focused on what could help me accomplish that basic goal consistently. Through a lot of trial, error and prototype putters, I created a unique new way to putt: the LEAN LOCK™ putting method. It combines a unique way of holding the putter with patent-pending putter features designed to make it all work together.

Putting is the part of the game requiring the least amount of physical strength, flexibility, or athleticism. Any golfer, and I mean ANY golfer, has the physical ability to be a good, if not excellent, putter. It helps tremendously if you understand what the putter must do during the stroke to strike a pure putt and you use a putting method that enables you to do it consistently, with the smallest margin of error. That is what this book is about. Read it and you will understand how to strike a pure putt and how the LEAN LOCK™ putting method will help you do it consistently.

INTRODUCTION

Let's get this out of the way right up front. There is a big difference between *sinking* putts and *striking pure putts*. While the overall goal is obviously to sink putts, if you do not read the speed and break correctly, and match the two up properly, you are unlikely to sink a putt even if your putting stroke is perfect, and you strike the putt pure. This book focuses only on helping people learn how to strike pure putts more consistently.

All great putters strike the majority of their putts pure, meaning they get the ball rolling immediately end over end, starting where they intended it to start. They also read greens well which is a learned skill, and an entire book could be written on that subject alone. To summarize it, reading greens is the ability to analyze and interpret the different slopes and grass conditions to determine how those will impact the speed and direction(s) the ball will move on its way to the target. Properly judging those conditions and having good visualization capabilities helps you decide where to aim. That is what reading greens is really about. Far too many people believe and exclaim, "I misread it," almost every time they miss a putt. That might have been the case, but it was most likely only part of the reason why the putt was missed. The majority of golfers I see actually miss-hit almost every putt. That causes the ball to roll differently than they intended which is the real reason they miss so many putts.

Once you consistently strike most of your putts pure, your ability to read greens improves dramatically. Reading greens well and striking pure putts go hand in hand. When you are striking pure putts the feedback you are getting is perfectly accurate. If a putt struck purely went too long or short and/or missed left or right, you know it was your speed control or your read of the amount of break which caused it to happen. This allows you to better adjust on the next putt and as your round progresses. Conversely, if you are unknowingly miss-hitting putts - causing them to come up short, miss left or miss right - you will make unnecessary adjustments to your speed or aim on your next putt and the ball will miss, but you will not understand why. Once you learn to consistently strike pure putts, you will be getting accurate feedback and your ability to read greens will improve.

ONE

THREE KEYS TO STRIKING A PURE PUTT

Here is a trick question for you: what do pizza and putting have in common? When I thought about writing this section the first thing that came to my mind was the similarity between the concept of striking a pure putt and running a profitable pizza restaurant. That might sound strange but hear me out. When I worked in the restaurant industry as a franchisee and executive at Papa John's (Pizza) International, we used to say there are only three things you need to do to run a successful restaurant: provide good food, good service and do it at a reasonable price. That sounds simple, but a lot of restaurateurs can attest it is not always easy. The same thing could be said about striking a pure putt. It is a simple motion, but there are a lot of frustrated golfers that will tell you it is not easy. Franchising provides a system and method to follow to make running a successful Papa John's Pizza restaurant easier to do with a higher likelihood of success. Similarly, the LEAN LOCK™ putting method is a system that makes striking pure putts simpler and easier to do.

Striking a pure putt means *hitting a putt that starts the ball rolling end over end immediately in the direction you intended for it to start;* that's it. No matter how you accomplished it, if you do that you have hit the putt "pure" and have achieved the goal of your putting stroke. Reading the green, aiming the putter face and hitting it the correct speed for the line you have chosen are important for sinking putts, but they have nothing to do with whether or not you have struck the putt "pure." When judging your putting, be careful not to confuse the difference between sinking putts and striking putts pure.

There are only three factors affecting how the ball rolls off the putter face when it strikes the ball.[1] In order to strike a perfectly pure putt all three need to be executed correctly. They are:

1. **The direction the club face is aimed at the moment of impact**

2. **The path of the club head as it approaches and impacts the ball**

3. **The attack angle at which the putter approaches and strikes the ball**

I call those three elements the "**APA**," which stands for club face **A**im, club head **P**ath and **A**ttack angle. Execute the Aim, Path and Attack angle (APA) properly and you will strike every putt pure.

---

[1] It is important your putter has the correct lie and loft angles to suit your impact conditions. All LEAN LOCK™ Putters are designed and built with the proper loft and lie angle specifically for the LEAN LOCK™ putting method. No other putters are designed for or appropriate for using the LEAN LOCK™ putting method. For purposes of this book, we have assumed your putter has the correct amount of loft and the correct lie angle so we do not discuss it as a point of concern when referring to the factors necessary to strike pure putts.

We all see the advertisements for new clubs, including putters, which claim to miraculously correct or at least minimize the error caused by our miss-hits. There is some truly wonderful technology that can improve our miss-hits, but shouldn't we start by learning how to strike pure putts and minimize the number of miss-hits in the first place? I created the LEAN LOCK™ putting method to help golfers strike more pure putts and enjoy the game of golf more.

LEAN LOCK PUTTING

SHIP TO

James Taylor
Jimmy Taylor Publishing
165 Good Hope Rd
–
Okatie SC 29909
United States
(843) 815-3211

BILL TO

James Taylor
Jimmy Taylor Publishing
165 Good Hope Rd
–
Okatie SC 29909
United States

ITEMS	QUANTITY
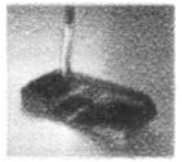 LEAN LOCK Blade Putter with Bonus LEAN LOCK Putting Book Blade 43"	1 of 1

Thank you for shopping with us!

Lean Lock Putting
9 OAK POINT DRIVE, FERNANDINA BEACH FL 32034, United States
info@leanlockputting.com
leanlockputting.com

TWO

CLUB FACE AIM AT IMPACT

The direction you intend for the ball to go when it first starts rolling is called the *"intended start line"* (ISL). The club face needs to be "square" to (pointed at) the *intended start line* at impact for the ball to roll perfectly in that direction. The direction the club face points at impact is by far the most important influencer of the direction the ball rolls. This point cannot be over-emphasized. Extensive research has been done using high-tech cameras and advanced computer technology to understand what happens when a golf club, in this case the putter, strikes the ball. The research indicates that 80% or more of the direction the ball travels is related to this one impact condition. There is no doubt it is the single most important thing we need to do in order to strike pure putts. Conquering it will put you well on your way to becoming a great putter.

Face rotation, the amount the face of the putter opens relative to where it was aimed during the back swing and closes during the forward swing, plays a big role in our ability to consistently return the putter face to square at impact. It stands to reason the less face rotation there is the easier it is to return the face to square at impact. For instance, if one player has 5 degrees of face rotation during the back swing and another has 15 degrees, the player with only 5 degrees has a much better chance of returning the face back to square at impact.

If you are still wondering why reducing face rotation is beneficial, consider this: if the putter face is 0.5 degrees or fewer, open or closed, when returned to impact, a 15-foot putt will still go in the hole. Conversely, increase to just 2.0 degrees open or closed at impact and even a 5-foot putt will miss. Controlling where the club face is aimed at the moment of impact is critically important.

Without any conscious effort or manipulation, the LEAN LOCK™ putting method reduces the amount of face rotation likely to occur during the putting stroke; making it more likely you will return the club face square and aimed along the intended start line at impact. Testing of the LEAN LOCK™ putting method using the SAM PuttLab video and software system proves how well it works in limiting club face rotation. The following screenshots are from one of my personal testing sessions.

As noted in Illustration 1 on the opposite page, the SAM PuttLab system measures the face aim *at a relative basis* to where the camera is placed (calibrated). They are telling us the camera may not be set up exactly square to the intended start line, which is the hole on a straight putt. For this discussion, where the face is aimed at address establishes the baseline for determining how much the face aim has changed at impact relative to where it started at address. Perfection would be for the putter face at impact to point exactly where it was aimed at address, resulting in a 0.0-degree difference between the two.

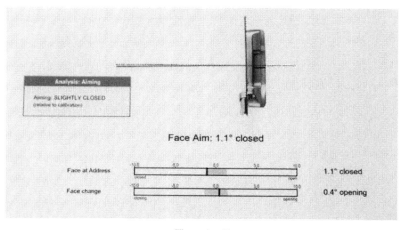

(Illustration 1)

During this putting session, Illustration 1 shows the putter face was aimed 1.1 degrees closed *relative to the camera* at address. The box at the bottom of the first screenshot labeled "face change," indicates the face was 0.4 degrees different (more open) at the moment of impact compared to where it was aimed at address. Illustration 2 shows that in a different way. It shows the face was 0.7 degrees closed *relative to the camera* at impact after being 1.1 degree closed *relative to the camera* at address; a difference of only 0.4 degrees.

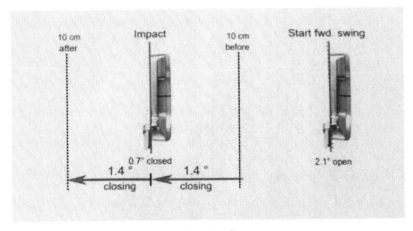

(Illustration 2)

Remember, a 15-foot putt will go in as long as the face is less than 0.5 degrees open or closed at impact. In my testing of the LEAN LOCK™ putting method, compared to where I aim it the putter face is consistently less than 0.5 degrees different at impact. During the putting session represented in these screenshots the average difference was only 0.4 degrees. Not surprisingly, I sank 20-25 consecutive putts from approximately 15 feet during that session.

Illustration 2 also confirms two other positive attributes of using the LEAN LOCK™ putting method: total face rotation and rate of rotation. On the far right it shows at the start of the forward swing, which is also the completion of the back swing, the club face was 2.1 degrees open *relative to the camera* at approximately 20 centimeters (about 8 inches) behind the ball. Since the face was 1.1-degree closed *relative to the* camera at address, the face rotated 3.2 degrees open at the completion of the back swing compared to where it was aimed at address. That is very minimal face rotation; in fact, it is notably less than the average collegiate golfer and in line with the best PGA Tour players[2]. The numbers and arrows at the bottom are measurements of the amount of face rotation during the most critical final 10 cm (about 4 inches) leading up to impact and during the first 10 cm after impact. While what occurs after impact has no influence on where the ball travels, the perfectly symmetrical rate of face rotation of just 1.4 degrees both before and after impact indicates there were no abrupt movements such as breaking down of the wrists or manipulation by the hands. With only 1.4 degrees of face rotation during the final 10 cm leading up to impact, a 5-foot putt struck anywhere in that roughly 4-inch area would still go in the hole. This SAM PuttLab data indicates the LEAN LOCK™ putting method minimizes face rotation, increasing the golfer's ability to return the club face to square at impact.

---

[2] According to data collected by PGA Professional and Lead Putting Instructor at TPC Sawgrass, Mike Shannon, PGA Tour Professionals typically range between 3 and 6 degrees of rotation during the back swing and the average collegiate players average 12-14 degrees.

THREE

CLUB HEAD PATH

The path the putter head takes during the stroke may be the most talked about component in golf putting instruction, and it is another important element of striking pure putts. Never-ending arguments are made about whether the putting stroke should be on what is commonly known as a "straight back / straight through" path, remaining as close to the *intended start line* as possible at all times, or should follow an "arc," traveling inside the *intended start line* during the back swing, back to "square" at the moment of impact and then slightly inside the *intended start line* after impact. Fortunes have been made by instructors teaching one method versus the other and "proving" for various reasons why one is superior to the other. I prefer referring to the straight-back-straight-through approach as straight-back-straight-<u>forward</u> or "**SBSF,**" because it better describes that the putter head should travel on a path straight along the *intended start line* for the entirety of the forward swing, not just the through swing after impact.

Regardless of which concept you think is best, the primary goal is to send the ball rolling instantly end over end directly along the *intended start line* we have chosen. To do that perfectly, **slightly before and at the moment of impact, the putter must be traveling along an extension of the *intended start line* with a**

club face that is square to it. In Chapter Two, we discussed the importance of club face aim and the critical effect it has on where the ball goes. In this chapter, we will discuss the importance of the path of the putter head.

As the putter approaches and impacts the ball, if it is traveling on a path from the inside of the *intended start line* and moving toward the outside, the force applied to the ball by a right-handed golfer will be toward the right of the *intended start line.* Depending on where the club face is pointed, that will tend to make the ball start to the right of where it's intended. Alternatively, if the putter is traveling on a path from the outside of the *intended start line* and moving toward the inside, the force applied to the ball by a right-handed golfer will be toward the left of where it's intended. Depending on where the club face is pointed, that will tend to make the ball start to the left of where it's intended.

As shown in Illustration 3, my testing of the LEAN LOCK™ putting method using the SAM PuttLab technology to measure the path the putter head takes during the back swing and then forward back into the ball at impact confirms it produces an excellent putter head path.

(Illustration 3)

The black square is the ball, the thicker dotted line represents the back swing path, and the solid line represents the forward swing path. The thinner dotted line extending farthest to the right represents an extension of the intended start line directly behind the ball and post impact. The putter has traveled so consistently straight back and straight forward that it is almost difficult to distinguish the back swing line from the forward swing line. This is the ideal scenario for consistency and will result in smaller misses even when your stroke is not quite as perfect as you would like for it to be.

If you remain unconvinced that the two most important factors determining where the ball goes are: (1) where the club face points at impact and, (2) the path the putter is traveling slightly prior to and at the moment of impact, consider how strongly the USGA and R&A feel about it. As the official governing bodies of golf worldwide, they have created extensive rules and regulations restricting the design attributes of putters along with outlawing certain putting methods which they deem to create an unfair advantage. Based on their own research, the USGA created many of those restrictions because they clearly believe some things makes it too easy to swing the putter on a straight-back / straight-forward path, and in their view, too easy to return the putter's face back to the ball in a "square" position. Those rules and restrictions are a clear indication the USGA and R&A believe that using an SBSF method, with little or no rotation of the putter face during the stroke is a superior way to putt. The LEAN LOCK™ putting method is specifically designed to create a SBSF path with very little face rotation.

FOUR

ANGLE OF ATTACK

The final "A" in the APA stands for the **attack** angle. In my opinion it is the most ignored and least understood element of striking pure putts. The angle of attack, combined with the amount of effective loft on the putter at impact, plays a critical role in getting the ball rolling end over end as soon as possible. If the ball is not rolling, it is either launched into the air or driven down into the ground causing it to bounce. That makes it more difficult to predict or control both the distance and direction the ball will travel.

Don Bisesi, the PGA Professional at the municipal course I grew up playing in Evansville, Indiana, was watching me practice my putting one day during my best putting season on the PGA Tour. At that time, I was intentionally striking putts with an ascending angle into the ball. Don described the attack angle of my putter as being similar to an airplane taking off on a runway - traveling very low for a while as it begins forward and then very gradually inclining and moving upward as it takes off (impact). That is a good image to keep in mind to help you create this key attribute in your own stroke.

I mentioned previously the term "effective loft" so I want to make sure to clarify what that means. It is actually quite simple. Putters are designed to have the bottom of the putter, at the leading edge, resting flat to the playing surface when addressing the ball. They also have a small amount of loft built into the face of the putter; usually around 3-4 degrees when the putter is in that "as-designed" address position. However, golfers do not always return the putter face to impact with the exact same amount of loft the manufacturer built into it.

The "effective loft" is simply a measurement of the amount of loft the face of the putter has at the moment it strikes the ball. If the shaft is leaning further ahead at impact than at address, the putter will have reduced loft at the moment of impact. Conversely, the putter can have greater loft at impact than it had at address. This happens when the amount of hinge angle in the lead wrist changes (increases) during the stroke; which is commonly referred to as "breaking down."

Ideally, the putter should be ascending at an upward attack angle of 2 to 3 degrees as it impacts the ball. Combined with 1 to 4 degrees of "effective loft" at impact, that is just enough to lift the ball onto the top of the putting surface and start it rolling end over end instantly without any backspin or bouncing.

The SAM PuttLab data in Illustration 4 documents excellent angle of attack and impact conditions. It shows an attack angle rising slightly at impact combined with a small amount of effective loft on the putter face, creating neutral spin for a pure roll. The LEAN LOCK™ putting method is designed to produce these conditions.

Illustration 5 is a side view showing the height of the putter head as it travels during the forward swing (from right to left) into and past the ball on ten different putts. Note how the lines indicate the putter head traveled close to the ground as it approached the ball, which is represented by the black dot. It starts moving upward just prior to impact, similar to an airplane speeding up and lifting off a runway, just like my childhood pro said. Thanks, Don!

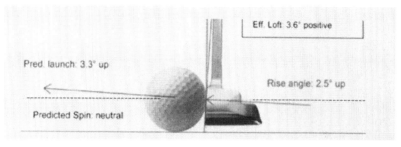

(Illustration 4)

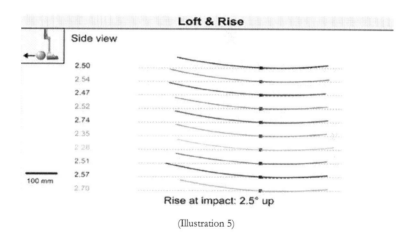

(Illustration 5)

FIVE

GRIPPING THE PUTTER

In this section you will learn step-by-step how to properly grip/hold a LEAN LOCK™ putter and a setup routine that will make doing it second nature very quickly. This method of gripping the club eliminates any possibility of the lead wrist "breaking down" toward the target during the stroke. **Even if you disagree with the methods espoused in this book regarding setup, alignment and path/shape of the stroke, adopting this gripping method with a Lean Lock™ putter will eliminate the problem of the wrists breaking down during the putting stroke.**

This unique method for gripping and holding the putter requires using a patent-pending putter designed unlike any other, and results in a visual appearance unlike any other putter when addressing the ball. The most striking difference is the putter has much more forward shaft lean angle than other putters when the bottom of the putter is resting as it is designed to be, flat to the playing surface. The innovative and patent-pending attributes of LEAN LOCK™ Putters, including the extreme amount of forward shaft lean, are an integral and critical aspect of using the LEAN LOCK™ putting grip. No other putters are manufactured to allow golfers to grip the putter this way while maintaining the correct amount of effective loft at impact.

The SAM PuttLab data shown in Chapter Two confirms the LEAN LOCK™ putting method and grip, when used with a LEAN LOCK™ Putter, consistently produces the three key conditions (APA) necessary to strike pure putts. It creates "locks" that eliminate many common faults that cause golfers to hit poor putts. When using this method the wrists cannot "break down" at impact, and any tendency to do so will actually strengthen the locking effect. That greatly reduces the potential amount of face rotation and potential for undesirable changes in loft occurring at impact.

I recommend placing your hands using the same overlap grip commonly used when hitting full golf shots (Images 1 & 2) as opposed to the "reverse-overlap" grip that is often used for putting. That being said, use whatever is most comfortable as long as it allows you to achieve the prescribed relationships and angles.

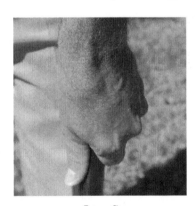

(Image 1)   (Image 2)

READER'S NOTE: For the remainder of the book the terms 'lead' or 'leading' refer to the side closest to the target, which is the left side for a right-handed golfer and the right side for a left-handed golfer. The terms 'trail' or 'trailing' refer to the side furthest from the target, which is the right side for a right-handed golfer and the left side for a left-handed golfer.

STEP 1.

For a right-handed golfer, while resting your lead hand and arm at your side and the right elbow slightly bent, hold the putter with your trail hand only; low on the grip with the shaft running straight up through the middle of the palm in-line with the forearm. Simultaneously aim the putter face on the line you want to start the ball rolling. As will be discussed in greater detail in Chapter Six, doing this with the feet and shoulders aligned and open (pointed left), relative to where you are aiming (the "Intended Start Line" or "ISL"), is recommended.

(Image 3)   (Image 4)

When done correctly with the putter head resting flat on the playing surface, the shaft will be leaning toward the target and the back of the trailing wrist will be hinged back, away from the target and away from the shaft. You "lean" the putter to start in Step 1, before you "lock it" in Steps 2 and 3.

The trailing elbow should be somewhat bent, not fully extended, so that the shaft and forearm will be in line with each other on the same lie angle when viewing them from along the target line, as illustrated in Images 4 and 5.

(Image 5)

STEP 2.

Keeping your lead shoulder low and relaxed, and the elbow bent, move your lead arm into a position where the shaft is on the target side of the arm and the forearm is in line with the shaft.

(Image 6)

(Image 7)

STEP 3.

Grip the club with your lead hand, placing it in an exaggerated "strong" position. The thumb should rest approximately at a 45-degree offset to the club face, on the side opposite the target. When using a LEAN LOCK™ Putter, the thumb will rest on the flat side of the grip, which is uniquely installed for maximum comfort and as a reminder where to place your thumb. While doing this, position the shaft so the flat, upper portion of the butt-end of the grip is located and secured against the <u>target side</u> of your lead forearm, <u>not</u> <u>underneath</u> the forearm. When gripping it properly you should be able to see all four knuckles of the left hand when looking down. The top of the lead wrist above the thumb should be bowed downward as highlighted with the line in Image 9.

(Image 8)

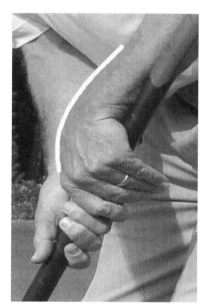

(Image 9)

STEP 4.

You should be able to hold the club securely by applying pressure with only the thumb of the lead hand. Test the grip by completely removing the pinky and middle two fingers of the lead hand from the shaft. Applying pressure with the lead hand's thumb should increase the pressure of the shaft against the target side (outside) of your arm, to the extent that you can even choose to leave those three fingers off the club while you strike putts. I prefer leaving those three fingers off the club when I putt to avoid creating excess tension in the left hand and side.

STEP 5.

Place the palm of your trail hand back in the position it held in Step 1, facing the ISL, but this time place it on top of the thumb of the lead hand instead of directly against the shaft. The shaft and lead hand thumb should run up through the palm and lifeline of the trail hand. I recommend using the same overlap grip or interlocking grip you use on your full swing shots, not the popular "reverse-overlap" grip often recommended for putting.

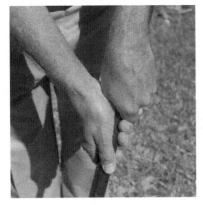

(Image 10)

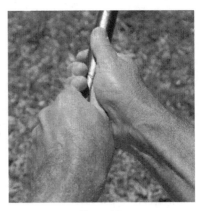

(Image 11)

When you have completed gripping the club, the trail arm's elbow should be slightly bent. When it is bent and positioned correctly, the trailing forearm will be directly in line with the angle of the shaft when viewing the setup along the ISL away from the target. In fact, both forearms are in line with the angle of the shaft. That alignment places the force of energy you apply directly in line with the object you are swinging (the shaft). It is an important checkpoint that can be seen in Image 12.

(Image 12)

Key angles and pressure points to "Triple-Lock" your grip when holding the club properly:

a. The thumb and index finger are the main controllers of the lead hand grip. Pressure should be applied by the lead hand's thumb against the grip, pushing it forward, while the index finger pinches the shaft from the opposite side. The other fingers of the lead hand, if on the club at all, are relaxed.

b. As a result of the pressure applied to the shaft by the lead hand's thumb in item "a," you should feel the upper end of the grip pushing against the upper, target side portion of the lead forearm, effectively locking the shaft against the arm (lock #1). If you do not feel that pressure and connection, the shaft is likely angled too low and underneath the forearm instead of positioned more upright on the lead/target-side edge of it. Too little bend in the elbow makes it difficult to achieve this position properly.

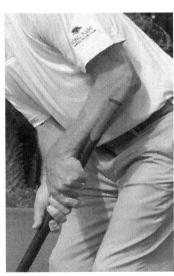

(Image 13)

c. There should be a feeling of stretching or pressure at the edge of the lead wrist just above the thumb. It should feel as if the pressure applied by the lead thumb has angled the pinky finger side of that lead wrist forward (called "ulnar deviation"), so much that it feels it is locked in that position (lock #2). If you cannot feel that or cannot see all four knuckles of the lead hand when looking down at your grip while addressing the ball, the grip is too weak and should be strengthened (rotated farther away from the target), and the hand below the joint on the pinky side of the wrist should be angled farther forward.

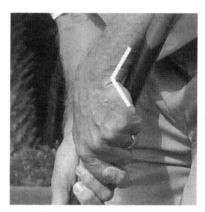

(Image 14)

d. Except for the index finger and thumb, which pinch the shaft, the fingers of the trail hand should be relaxed, resting gently on the grip. It is the thumb and index finger of the trail hand that provide the feel and "touch" you have developed over your lifetime; similar to throwing a dart at a dart board or picking a coin up off of a table. You should feel only light pressure in the palm of the trail hand onto the lead hand's thumb as it runs directly through the lifeline of the trailing hand's palm. Throughout the stroke, the pressure applied by the trailing thumb, index finger and palm, should remain constant.

e. When addressing the ball, the back of the trail wrist should be bent/hinged back on itself without any forearm rotation. The palm should be facing the ISL and the knuckles should point backward along it (called "wrist extension"). The angle created at address should remain intact during the stroke due to the pressure applied in "d" above (lock #3).

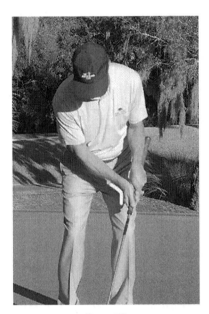

(Image 15)

f. Check again and make sure that **the lead elbow is significantly bent and close to the side.** The lead shoulder is relaxed and hanging, not lifted up. As a result, the upper portion of the lead arm is close to the torso at address, almost touching it (Image 16). These are very important positions. **Resist the temptation to straighten the lead arm, move it away from your body, or point the elbow toward the target.**

(Image 16)

SIX

ADDRESSING THE BALL

The LEAN LOCK™ putting method is based on the trailing hand/side being the "fulcrum" that swings the putter and dominates the stroke, which means the right hand, arm and shoulder are doing most of the work to control the stroke and control the speed for a right-handed golfer. With the trail hand and forearm in alignment with the shaft at address they operate like a piston during the putting stroke to propel the putter head straight along an extension of the *intended start line*. This might sound strange to those who are arc method putters or compared to most current putting instruction, but the benefits of doing this were clear in the SAM PuttLab session data presented earlier. In addition, some of the best putters of all time including Jack Nicklaus, have mentioned this as a key concept.

The positions in which you align your body relative to the target, and relative to the ball, play an important role in determining the path of your stroke and the amount of face rotation you have relative to the *intended start line (ISL)* during the stroke. The PGA Tour pros you see on television are meticulous about it. You too should develop a consistent set-up routine. Developing a routine like the one described in the following steps will help you develop a consistent LEAN LOCK™ setup, and your putting consistency will quickly improve as a result.

STEP 1.

Follow the steps in Chapter Five to grip the club and settle your body into a comfortable posture. Aim the face of your putter on the line you want the ball to start. Practice aiming often and use whatever aides you need to learn to aim correctly (e.g., using a line on the ball). I recommend aiming the putter while maintaining "open" shoulders and an "open" stance; where the lead side is farther away from the *intended start line* than the trailing side, and the lead foot is flared to point slightly toward the target.

(Image 17)

Regardless of where the feet are aligned, the eyes should be positioned directly over an extension of the ISL at address. Eyes that are inside the ISL, a common error, make aiming more difficult and encourages the path of the putter to be to the inside instead of SBSF. It will also encourage excess face rotation. Your dominant eye should be positioned either directly over the ball itself or slightly behind it and above the ISL. As a checkpoint, if you dropped a ball from just below your dominant eye, it would either hit the ball on the ground or land on an extension of the ISL just behind it. Never position your dominant eye in front of the ball.

(Image 18)

(Image 19)

While the stance width and alignment can be varied based on personal comfort, in my opinion there is only one way to properly align your shoulders to encourage a natural straight-back-straight-forward stroke and get the full benefit of the LEAN LOCK™ putting method. To do that, ***the shoulders must be aligned open to the ISL at address.*** That is because the body is built for the shoulders to turn around and perpendicular to the spine. By aligning the shoulders in an open position to the ISL, when they move slightly "around" the spine the putter will travel straight back along the ISL for quite a long time instead of to the inside of it on an arc. The open shoulder set up position promotes a SBSF path without any conscious effort. It also creates more room for the dominant trail hand/arm/shoulder to operate like a piston and swing directly along the ISL during the forward swing until just past the point of impact.

Do not worry too much about what the lead side is doing after you have set up to the ball. Its main purpose is to stabilize the putter by locking the lead wrist and locking the putter to the lead arm. During the stroke the lead side should be noticeably relaxed. Pay attention to make sure it is.

While I do not recommend it, some golfers say it helps to feel like the shoulders control their stroke. If you are one of them and choose to do that, make sure to feel as if the lead shoulder is pushing the putter head down to start the back swing so that the putter head moves back low and along the ISL. To the extent the lead shoulder does move while making the stroke, you should strive to feel like it moves "down" on the backswing and then "up" during the forward swing. No matter how you feel you control the putter best, make sure the "hit" or "tap" at impact comes distinctly from the trailing hand. That is where your natural touch comes from.

STEP 2.

Weight distribution at address is very important. It plays a big role in your balance and stability during the stroke and most importantly, it impacts the attack angle. I recommend your weight distribution at address be about 60% on your trail foot and 40% on the lead foot. How you accomplish that is important. To set yourself up to make an ascending angle of attack, I suggest you adopt what has long been referred to in golf as the "Reverse K" position. The "Reverse K" position with weight bias toward your trail foot will encourage the putter to go back low to the ground during the back stroke and begin ascending just prior to impact. That is the last key attribute of your APA: creating an ascending attack angle.

(Image 20)

To accomplish the "Reverse K," start with your weight equally distributed between your feet, then shift your hips an inch or two forward so the bottom point of your spine (at the hips), is further forward than the upper spine at the base of your neck (Image 21). Next, drop your trail shoulder and elbow lower without moving your head position. Doing those two things will shift the lower spine forward, tilt your upper spine slightly away from the target, and move about 10 percent of your weight to your trail foot. *The entire right side, especially the trailing elbow and shoulder, must feel and should be "low and underneath" relative to the lead side at address.* That is a critical position and checkpoint; so make sure you are in the correct position. Remember, this is accomplished by shifting the hips slightly forward and lowering the right shoulder and elbow, NOT by moving the left side/shoulder artificially higher.

(Image 21)   (Image 22)

SEVEN

————

PUTTING IT ALL TOGETHER

Putting requires controlling how the putter moves with precise "feel" for exactly how much force to apply. Luckily, those are the things you have unknowingly spent your entire life training yourself to know how to do without even thinking about it. It does not require strength, flexibility, or physical athleticism; just some hand-eye coordination and the proper setup position to allow it to happen.

Think about it. Whether right-handed or left-handed, we have spent a lifetime training our eyes, mind, dominant hand, and fingers to work together to do an incredible variety of things. It truly is remarkable what we have learned to do over a lifetime without consciously thinking about it. We have lifted, picked up, moved around, and even thrown different objects with accuracy such as baseballs, darts, basketballs, volleyballs or even trash into a wastebasket. We have learned to write our names, brush our teeth, shave, and pick up tiny objects without a moment's thought. Not only that, but we have developed a deft touch and the ability to apply the correct amount of force and direction with perfect precision in any number of situations. With a lifetime of training like that, why would we want to approach a task like putting a golf ball using only our "big muscles" or using the lead hand to "pull"? It does not make sense to do that. We should use our dominant trail hand, which we have spent a lifetime training, to control our putting.

The key to striking pure putts using the LEAN LOCK™ putting method is to allow yourself to trust your dominant side traits and the hand-eye coordination you have spent a lifetime developing. For a right-handed golfer, that is the right/trail hand, arm and shoulder. The left/lead side has been by design set up in an open position to be out of the way and not interfere. Except for the pressure points and locks created during the setup, the lead side should be relaxed and more or less along for the ride.

The putting stroke and your "touch" or "feel" are controlled by your dominant trail hand, arm, and shoulder. That concept is taboo in many of today's most popular putting theories and instruction. People fear the trailing dominant hand will overtake the lead hand, causing a breakdown in the wrists and loss of control over the putter face. The LEAN LOCK™ putting method eliminates the possibility of that breakdown due to the system of locks created in the setup. We are free to control the stroke and strike the ball using our dominant trailing hand/side without any fear. The right trail hand, forearm, and shoulder, combined with the putter, work as one single unit. If it helps, focusing on using one or the other, either the trailing shoulder or trailing hand is fine, but I prefer the hand since it has the most "feel." Experiment to determine which thought works best for you, but remember it is the trailing hand that has the most hand-eye coordination and "feel" or "touch" for distance control.

When you are ready to start the stroke, remember that controlling the APA is what produces a pure putt. Again, APA stands for your club face **Aim**, **P**ath and **A**ttack angle *at and just prior to the moment of impact.* The recommended setup position encourages the APA to happen correctly, but it is still important to understand what you want the putter head to do during the stroke.

We want the putter to travel as close to straight along an extension of the *intended start line* as possible at all times, both back and forward, especially slightly before and at the moment of impact, with a club face perfectly square to it, while striking the ball at an ascending upward angle.

There are a few critical things you should think about and make sure to do during the stroke to control your APA to the ultimate degree. These will need to be conscious thoughts as you are first learning the LEAN LOCK™ method but will become second nature and, like the gripping method, will occur naturally after a little practice. When you find your putting is a little off, these are the first things you should check:

1. **Take the putter back far enough, farther than you think.** Taking it back too short is the most common mistake. It causes a fast transition and abrupt acceleration.

2. **The head of the putter leads the backswing.** Push the head down and back, low to the ground.

3. **"Hit up" on the ball at impact.** It should feel like you are "tapping" the ball on an upward angle when you strike it.

4. **A slow transition is important.** The fastest point in the stroke is at the ball, not before or after that point.

Taking It Back Low Is Important

When it comes to controlling the APA, after setting up few things are more impactful than striving to have the putter head lead the way low to the ground during the back swing. That one concept will reduce club face rotation making it more likely to return to impact "square" (club face **a**im). It also encourages the **p**ath to remain directly along an extension of the ISL at all times, and it virtually guarantees a slightly ascending **a**ttack angle at impact. Jack Nicklaus and Lee Trevino both spoke about taking it back low as a key to good putting.

It should feel as though the trail hand (or shoulder, as preferred) is "pushing the putter head down and straight back" low and close to the ground along an extension of the ISL to start the back swing. That is how we make the putter head lead; meaning the putter head travels further than the butt end.

(Image 23)

As I said previously, some golfers tell me it is easier for them to feel like they push the head "down and straight back" with their lead shoulder or even with both shoulders as a unit. That is okay as long as you make the forward stroke with the dominant trail hand, which is how your natural "touch" and "feel" for how hard to strike the ball, will be most effective. Also be aware that using the lead shoulder as the dominant controller of the backswing can create unwanted tension in the left side and promote pulling the club through with a long follow through rather than the shorter and more aggressive "tap" we are looking for at the ball.

(Image 24)   (Image 25)

In Images 24 and 25, notice how the putter head has moved quite a distance back along the ISL while the grip end of the putter has not moved much at all. As a good reference point, in the photographs compare where the grip end of the putter is relative to the Spanish Moss in the background at address in Image 24 versus at the completion of the back swing in Image 25. The head has moved 12-14 inches while the end of the grip has moved only 3 to 4 inches. Yours should do the same.

With the putter head leading on the way back, low with very little face rotation, **it may feel like the putter face is pointed "down" toward the ground at a backward extension of the ISL during the back swing. When first making this change that position might feel "closed" or "shut" because most golfers typically have far too much face rotation ("opening") during the back swing. It is okay, perhaps even better, to feel like the face is slightly closed at that position.**

Take the Putter Back Far Enough

The length of the back swing is influenced by the tempo of the stroke. Faster tempo produces more power, so it requires a shorter back swing. Slower tempo is typically accompanied by a longer back swing. Everyone has a different tempo, so experiment to find the one that is comfortable for you. Practicing with a metronome is a good exercise to help you find your best tempo.

Regardless of your tempo, I cannot over-emphasize that having a back swing that is too short is much, much worse than a back swing you feel is too long. A back swing that is too short forces a rushed transition with acceleration too soon in the forward swing. That ruins distance control and puts torque on the putter face causing it to rotate, which you then need to counteract to strike a pure putt. Take the putter back far enough, farther than you think you should, on putts of every length. Remember this thought, "the **putter head leads**, going back **low and long**."

Upon completing the back swing and at the transition to making the forward swing, strive to *start the forward swing at the same speed as you completed the back swing.* Start at the speed you finish.

Good thoughts for the transition from back swing to forward swing should center on words like "slow" and "be patient." Similar to the airplane starting its takeoff from the end of the runway, we do not need rapid acceleration or speed at the beginning of the move forward; we need speed at impact when we strike the ball just like the airplane needs it to get off the ground. Start the forward swing slowly as though gravity is what makes the club start swinging forward. Only add the acceleration and speed/force you need when the putter head reaches the ball. That is done with your trailing dominant hand to gain the most benefit from the sense of "feel" and "touch" you have developed over your lifetime. Adding the speed just prior to and at impact, instead of beginning at the transition to the forward swing, will feel as if you are distinctly "hitting" or perhaps "tapping" the ball at impact. This is what you want to feel! The fastest point in the stroke should be at the ball, not before it or past it.

After the Strike

With a back swing that is low and long enough, starting the forward swing at the same speed as you completed the back swing, and an upward "hit" or "tap" at impact, post impact is simply a result of everything else we have done. The through stroke has nothing to do with where the ball goes. The ball is only touching the club face for a microsecond before it is gone and on its way. Why would we care about what the club face is doing or where it goes once the ball is already on its way? You should not, except for the feedback it provides about how well you executed the other aspects of the putting stroke.

Here is what to look for after the strike and at completion of the stroke in order to learn from it. These checkpoints can be a valuable tool to help you correct your stroke quickly when your putting gets off track:

1) If the putter face is rotated overly closed after impact rather than remaining relatively close to square, there was likely too much face rotation both in the back and forward swings.

2) The putter should finish relatively high, much higher than the back swing, which is indicative of an ascending attack angle.

3) The through stroke after impact should be relatively short, definitely *not longer than* the length of the back swing and ideally one-half or less the length of the back swing. The length of the through swing confirms whether we made a back swing that was long enough, had the proper transition tempo and the correct amount of speed and "hit" at the ball. A through swing that is longer than the back swing indicates that the back swing was too short and over-acceleration probably occurred. In my experience, as long as the forward swing starts at the same speed as the back swing finishes and your ball rolls the distance you intended, there is no such thing as a through swing that is too short.

The Correct Putting Sequence – Down the Line

(Image 26)

(Image 27)

(Image 28)

This is a down-the-line sequence of a 15-foot putt. The hole is the dark spot at the end of the line. Note the open stance and the putter traveling low to the ground exactly along an extension of the intended start line both directions. There is an ascending angle of attack resulting in the putter finishing high off the ground with a short through stroke.

The Correct Putting Sequence – Face On

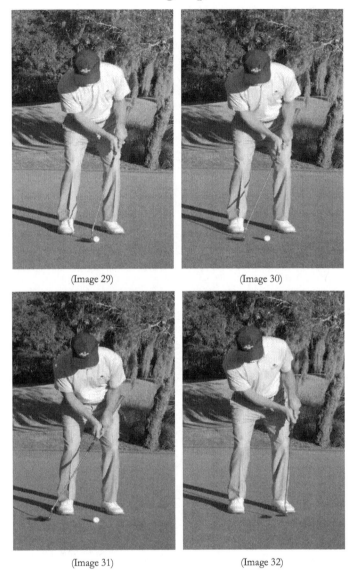

(Image 29) (Image 30)

(Image 31) (Image 32)

The putter head leads the way back, traveling low with minimal face rotation. The putter head approaches and impacts the ball on an ascending angle. It finishes high with a square club face, indicating minimal face rotation on the forward stroke as well.

The angles locked in at address are maintained throughout the entire putting stroke, and especially from the setup position back to impact. Image 33 below illustrates that very well. The center line represents address, the leftmost line is at completion of the back swing and the rightmost line represents the finish position. Note how the height of the corner of the angle of the lines moves lower during the back swing and is higher post-impact, documenting the ascending attack angle. Perfect!

(Image 33)

EIGHT

———

HOW TO PRACTICE

Any putting method can produce good results if you practice it enough to ingrain the feelings and keep those feelings fresh every day, but how many of us really have the time to do that or want to stand on the putting green for an hour or two at least several days a week to be a consistent putter? PGA Tour pros like Tiger Woods are famous for "putting in the reps," but most of us would rather be doing something else, not to mention bending over for long periods of time while practicing, can be hard on the back. With the LEAN LOCK™ putting method those days can be gone forever. Like I have, you can become a consistently good, if not great, putter by learning to set up properly and using a few simple training drills. You will groove a stroke that produces all the elements of the APA necessary to strike pure putts. I have even stopped taking practice strokes before I putt during a round. I don't need to loosen up for a putt and what is the point of taking a practice stroke when you know with a high degree of confidence you are going to strike the putt purely and start it online every time? I visualize the line and speed I want, then trust my lifetime of hand-eye training with my dominant hand to hit it the right speed.

In this chapter, we will cover several simple practice drills to help you groove your new LEAN LOCK™ putting stroke and periodically check to make sure the three elements of your APA are under control. The drills can be done individually or combined together.

Eye & Ball Position

In Chapter Six, I recommended positioning your eyes directly over an extension of the ISL at address with your dominant eye either directly over the ball or slightly behind it. As a checkpoint, while addressing the ball, if you dropped another ball from just below your dominant eye it would either hit the ball on the ground or land on an extension of the ISL just behind it. *Never position your dominant eye in front of the ball.*

How do we know which eye is dominant? Pick out an object in the distance and with both eyes open point your index finger at the object. Next close only your right eye while leaving the left eye open, and then reverse the process. Whichever eye is open when your finger remains pointed at the object is your dominant eye.

The best way to check and practice positioning your eyes correctly is to place a small mirror immediately behind the ball or use a training tool that has a built-in mirror. When looking down at the ball from the address position your eyes should be visible in the mirror, directly over the ISL, and your dominant eye should be either directly over the ball or behind it.

Keep Your Eyes Still

Keeping the eyes perfectly still while putting is absolutely essential and will help make a lot of other good things happen. Allowing them to wander will create a wide range of problems. If you move your eyes while putting it is all but impossible to strike a pure putt. Pick one specific spot for your eyes to focus on for the entirety of the stroke (e.g., the front or back of the ball, a spot just in front of the ball, or even the hole) and keep them locked there until the ball is well on its way. I focus my eyes on the back edge of the ball. To train my eyes to stay locked there, during practice sessions I place a small coin or ball marker underneath the back of the ball so that only a portion of it is visible from the address position. When striking the putt, I keep my eyes focused on that coin where the back edge of the ball originally was. I make sure to keep them there at least until the ball is on its way and I can see the entire coin or marker clearly before allowing my eyes to look up. Ideally, you should wait even longer, and the ball should disappear from your peripheral vision before the eyes move. In their prime, Nick Faldo and Tiger Woods did that very noticeably.

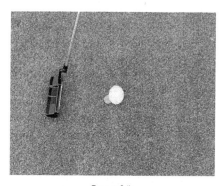

(Image 34)

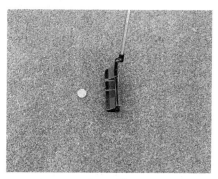

(Image 35)

Dominant Side Control

The trailing hand and side should be dominant while the lead hand and arm are relaxed and locked in place to create stability. To reinforce that, practice striking putts using only the trailing hand /side with the lead hand removed from the putter. Remember to focus on leading the stroke with the putter head - going back low, straight, far enough and "hitting up" on the ball with a short through swing. This will ingrain the correct feelings for controlling the stroke with your dominant hand and shoulder; with a smooth transition from back swing to forward swing.

(Image 36)

Taking the Putter Back Low

The benefits of taking the putter back low to the ground were described in Chapter Seven; including that the correct setup and weight distribution play a big role in achieving it. One way to check and practice taking it back low is to place two or three quarters stacked on top of each other about four to five inches behind the ball. The putter should knock the top quarter off of the pile on the back swing.

(Image 37)

(Image 38)

Long Back Swing, Short Through Swing

You can train yourself to have a long back swing, a short through swing, and a ratio between the two that is appropriate by using nothing more than a few golf tees. Start with a 6 to 8-foot putt. Referring to Images 39 and 40 below, create a "gate" by placing two tees in the ground about 2-3 inches in front of the ball with space just wide enough for the ball to pass through but narrow enough that the putter will not. Insert another tee in the ground *at least* 8-inches behind the ball (or more) directly on a backward extension of the ISL. Practice striking putts while stopping just short of the tee on the back swing and attempting to stop just short of the two tees in front of the ball on the forward swing. Do not worry if you hit the tees on the forward swing, at least initially, as it serves as a good reminder. Experiment with the exact placement of the tees based on the speed of the green, the length of the putt, and your tempo. Work to create a ratio of about 3:1 or 4:1 back compared to through. Always remember a longer back swing with a shorter through swing is the goal. As you master taking the putter back far enough, this drill will teach you to have a slow and smooth transition while feeling a "hit" or "tap" at the ball, which is where we want the fastest point of the stroke to be.

(Image 39)   (Image 40)

Straight-Back / Straight-Forward with Minimal Face Rotation

A proper setup while using the trail side hand and shoulder to control the stroke will go a long way toward producing an SBSF path. Making a back swing by leading with the putter head going back first, and very low, will help to minimize the face rotation. As a guide for your path, use a training aid or simply lay two golf clubs on the ground, parallel to and on each side of the ISL to form a track that is slightly wider than the width of your putter. The putter should stay in-between the two shafts at all times when making an SBSF stroke.

Hitting Up on the Ball

Learning to have an ascending attack angle will ensure the ball starts rolling instantly upon leaving the putter face. Once again, a proper setup and stroke, taking it back low, will encourage that to happen. To practice it, use an adaptation of the "quarter drill" used for taking it back low. In this case, place two stacks of four quarters each ($2.00 worth) even with the leading edge of the ball, one stack on the heel side and one on the toe side, less than the width of your putter apart. When making the correct ascending stroke, the putter will travel above the quarters leaving them undisturbed exactly where they started.

(Image 41)   (Image 42)

Learning How to Play Breaking Putts

With the LEAN LOCK™ putting method and making an SBSF stroke, every stroke should be identical except for its length and tempo to produce different speeds. Every putt is essentially played as a straight putt. We simply aim differently to account for the proper amount of break.

To train for this approach, find a putt on the practice green that has at least one to two cups of break at your chosen speed. Place a coin or ball marker down where you want to putt from so that you can hit from the same place every time, then insert a tee in the ground at the end of your *intended start line* about 12-18 inches past the back of the hole. Aim at the tee and strike putts while focusing on the tee as your target rather than the hole. The break will curve the ball into the hole even though you have struck a "straight" putt at the tee you placed in the ground. You can also use a chalk line or an elevated string as a visual aide for this training exercise.

(Image 43)   (Image 44)

Distance Control

Most of this book has been focused on how to control the variables to encourage and ensure you strike more putts pure with perfect APA. Distance control is not about mechanics, it is mostly art and "feel." In Chapter Seven, I made the argument that we have developed a terrific amount of feel and "touch" over our lifetime through our everyday activities. I believe that to be true, and by using the LEAN LOCK™ putting method, we have eliminated the mechanical putting thoughts that interfere with and inhibit our natural feel and "touch." We simply use our dominant, trailing hand to hit the ball the correct speed and distance based on what our eyes see and what our brain's analysis of the slope and turf conditions tells us to do.

When practicing distance control, do not use any stroke assistance devices or feedback aids like the ones discussed throughout this chapter. When practicing distance control, the goal is not to make a mechanically perfect stroke. We have taken care of that with our setup and the other practice drills. The goal is to learn to get our eyes in tune with what our brain sees in the slopes and turf conditions and to calibrate our brain's interpretation of those things for the greens we are playing. There is a way to practice that.

Find a putt of 30-feet in length between two holes on the practice green. Make sure it is at least slightly uphill one way, downhill the other, and has at least 1-2 feet of break each direction. Going through your full normal setup routine on every putt, strike three to five putts from one hole to the other, then go strike them back from that hole to the original hole. Make a game out of it. Depending on your skill level the goal is either to have every putt both reach the hole and stop no more than 2-3 feet past it, or alternatively, the goal can be simply for every ball to stop within a 2-3-foot circle around the hole in any direction. I prefer the first goal since every putt has a chance to go in and the margin of distance error is only two to three feet, training me to have more precise feel and control.

When working on the mechanics of your stroke, the APA, I do not recommend practicing putts longer than about 8-feet. When practicing distance control, I recommend you only practice putts of at least 30 feet or longer. Statistically, PGA Tour Pros on average make only about 71% of their putts from six feet. Granted, those are their putts under tournament conditions rather than in a static practice setting, but you get the point. Practicing from beyond 6-8 feet during APA practice is bound to lead to misses and hurt your confidence. We think we can and expect to make every 10, 15 or even 20-foot putt, but that is simply not going to happen. Practicing much longer putts of 30-plus feet in the manner I have suggested will help hone your feel and "touch." Do that and then go to the course and let your eyes and brain adapt to every other length and instinctively tell you how hard to strike it. In my mind, I say to myself "trust your eyes" and then I let the putt go. My playing partners often remark about how uncannily consistent my distance control is although it is something I rarely practice except for a few warm-up putts before each round to get a feel for the speed of the greens that particular day. Use this drill and that will soon be you.

NINE

QUICK TIPS AND COMMON ERRORS

One of the benefits of the LEAN LOCK™ putting method is once you have mastered the grip and setup routines there are only a few things that typically go wrong. That makes fixing your putting easier and faster when it is a little off. It also means the amount of practice time needed to be a great putter is dramatically reduced, which might be the biggest benefit. To help you fix yourself faster and stay on track with your putting, here are some quick tips and reminders:

Control your APA to hit pure putts. The three conditions that determine how the ball rolls off the putter face are:

1. **The direction the club face is aimed at the moment of impact**

2. **The path of the club head as it approaches and impacts the ball**

3. **The attack angle at which the putter approaches and strikes the ball**

The shaft runs up through the palm and lifeline of your trail hand, toward the forearm.

The trailing wrist has "wrist extension" at address.

The trailing forearm is in direct alignment with the shaft.

All four knuckles of the lead hand should be visible when looking down, if the grip is strong enough.

Use a "Reverse K" setup with 60% of the weight on the trail foot.

The shoulders should be open to the intended start line at address with the trailing elbow and shoulder feeling "underneath" and noticeably lower than the lead shoulder.

The lead elbow should be bent and near the body at address. The lead hand and shoulder should be relaxed and "along for the ride."

The trail hand, forearm and shoulder, combined with the putter, work as one single unit to control the stroke.

Lead the back swing with the putter head, moving it low to the ground and straight along an extension of the intended start line.

The butt/grip end of the club will travel very little; far less than the club head travels.

Take the putter back far enough. Longer is better.

If the ball is bouncing at the start on longer putts or you are consistently leaving putts short, a back swing that is too short is the most likely reason.

Strive to be "slow and patient" at the transition, starting the forward swing at the same speed as the back swing finished.

The stroke is fastest at impact. Acceleration occurs mainly just prior to and at impact, not sooner.

Feel as if you "hit up" on the ball with a "tap" at impact and a short follow-through.

——

TEN

DIFFERENT STROKES

If you made it this far you know I believe Straight-Back-Straight-Forward (SBSF) putting is the best approach. However, many of history's most successful professional golfers have utilized the concepts of the arc method with great success, and the Arm lock method is a popular recent trend. I thought it would be helpful to include some information on those other concepts.

Arc Putting

The main argument in favor of the arc putting concept is, similar to the full golf swing, the golfer is standing to the side of the golf ball at address so there is a natural tendency for the arms and club to travel around the torso to which they are attached, creating an arc. While traveling back along that arc during the back swing, the putter head will move to the inside of the *intended start line* and the face of the putter will appear to rotate in conjunction with the arc, which means at completion of the back swing the face of the putter is pointed some degree to the right of where you want the the putt to go. To whatever amount the putter head has traveled to the inside of the *intended start line* and to whatever degree the face is pointed to the right of it at completion of the back swing, the golfer must undo or retrace those changes perfectly by the moment of impact, in order to strike the ball with a square face and with the putter head traveling and applying force directly along the *intended start line*. There is only one infinitely small place and moment in time in an arc when a club traveling along an arc will have a face and path that are exactly square. That is at the exact bottom of the arc. Because of that, ball position is very important when using the arc concept and there is very little margin for error.

Proponents of arc putting argue anything other than an arc with face rotation proportionate to the arc requires manipulation by the golfer which leads to errors. Using high-tech video equipment, some of today's instructors and club fitters have measured and catalogued the putting strokes of hundreds of touring professionals and thousands of other golfers to create what they claim is the "optimum" amount of arc in the stroke combined with the "optimum" amount of face rotation. They then attempt to provide instruction on how to accomplish that, plus oftentimes recommend changing the loft, lie or type of putter the person is using.

As I see it, the problem with the arc concept is golfers have a difficult time controlling and consistently repeating the exact amount of arc (putter path) and exact amount of club face rotation (opening and closing) consistently enough to strike a pure putt, much less having the "optimum" amount. By and large, if you watch most average everyday golfers, you will quickly notice the majority have a large amount of face rotation during both the back swing and through swing and/or a path that travels neither on a true arc nor SBSF. All of those leads to poorly struck putts and inconsistency.

Another problem is figuring out what we are supposed to do in order to make that perfectly timed arc stroke happen. Do we control the stroke with our "big muscles" like the shoulders and back, with our left hand/arm, our right hand/arm? Do we have any forearm rotation, and should the wrists set or load to some degree and, if so, how much? For me, the combinations and potential for confusion goes on ad infinitum. I tried them all and many worked for a while, but every time my putting went south, I found I was confused and had difficulty getting my putting back on track. Add in nervousness or tension and the task becomes even more difficult.

If you putt using the arc methodology with a conventional gripping method, have consistent success, and do not think you can putt better than you currently do, please continue to use it. Everyone else, including myself, would benefit from using a simpler way to control the **APA** to more consistently strike pure putts.

Straight-Back / Straight-Forward

The tenets of the Straight-Back / Straight-Forward (SBSF) putting approach are diametrically opposed to the tenets of the arc stroke methodology. As the name implies, when using the SBSF concept the goal is to have the club head travel back and forward exactly along the *intended start line* of the putt with minimum face rotation. Ideally, the face of the putter remains pointed at an extension of the *intended start line* at all times.

Advocates of the SBSF method believe that the less the putter's path deviates from an extension of the intended start line during the stroke, the more likely it is to be traveling directly along it and propel the ball toward the intended start line when the putter impacts the ball. Logically, the less "arc" there is in the stroke, the more consistent your putting will be. The LEAN LOCK™ putting method was developed and designed to eliminate arc and create a path that is directly along an extension of the intended start line without the need for any conscious effort to make it happen.

Renowned putting and short game instructor, Dave Pelz, as well as others, have done extensive testing of the SBSF concept, even using machines to help test it. The data from those tests strongly suggests, if not completely proves, that if one can make the putter perform in this way the ball has a better chance of rolling where it is intended to go. It makes a lot of sense. Since we want the putter face to be square and the path to be directly along the *intended start line (ISL)* at the moment of impact, logically it is likely to happen more consistently if the club head path travels as close to the ISL as possible at all times and if the face rotates as little as possible during the stroke. Even if it is not done perfectly, less variation in the path and less putter face rotation should reduce the margin of error and lead to more consistency. Additionally, if our ball position varies it is less important since contact made within a wider area will start the ball close to along the ISL.

Arm lock

Advocates of the Arm lock gripping method are not strict about using an Arc stroke or an SBSF stroke. Bryson DeChambeau and Matt Kuchar are two opposing examples, but both use an Arm lock grip. The main argument for utilizing the Arm lock method is that it creates a connection between the shaft and the leading forward arm so as to help reduce the likelihood of the lead wrist breaking down at impact. It does that to some extent, but when compared to the LEAN LOCK™ putting method it is inferior in that respect. The LEAN LOCK™ method completely eliminates any possibility of the lead wrist breaking down at impact. The Arm lock method cannot make that claim.

The other drawback of the Arm lock method, in my experience and observation, is that it requires the golfer to apply significant pressure and tension with the lead hand, arm and even shoulder in order to keep the shaft connected to it. I believe that interferes with the golfer's athleticism, "feel," and "touch" that they have spent a lifetime developing in their trailing, dominant hand / side. In comparison, the LEAN LOCK™ method does a far superior job of locking the lead arm to the putter and does so with little lead side tension. LEAN LOCK™ allows the golfer to use their dominant, trail hand / side to control the stroke and exploit their lifetime of hand-eye coordination training with it to the fullest extent.

Claw/Pencil Grip Putting

Placing the dominant hand on the putter in this method was developed as a way to attempt to avoid the dominant hand from overtaking the lead hand during the stroke and causing the wrists to break down. In general, I don't have a problem with using the "Claw/Pencil" grip method of holding the putter with the dominant hand. However, when using the LEAN LOCK™ putting method, I don't see the benefit of it. The LEAN LOCK™ method completely eliminates the possibility of the dominant hand overtaking the lead hand and causing the lead wrist to break down so, for my money, I would rather fully utilize the lifetime of natural touch I have developed by placing my dominant hand in a more traditional position on the club when gripping it.

CONCLUSION

After a lifetime of inconsistency and struggles I am convinced the LEAN LOCK™ putting method is a superior way to consistently strike pure putts. It makes it easier to accomplish the APA by keeping the putter traveling very close to the intended start line for a long period of time with minimal face rotation and a slightly ascending attack angle, making it more likely to strike putts pure and sink more of them.

I hope this book helps you enjoy golf more by better understanding what must happen in order to strike a pure putt. More than that, my hope is that you now see the benefits of using the LEAN LOCK™ method. It will improve your putting and enable you to fix it quickly when it is not quite where you want it to be.

For me and the many people who have adopted it, the LEAN LOCK™ method has made the game easier and more fun. Our scores are lower and in golf, that's what matters most. Adopt it and follow the system detailed in this book and I'm confident you will have the same results. Visit **www.leanlockputting.com** to learn more and purchase your new LEAN LOCK™ putter to get started today!

ACKNOWLEDGEMENTS

Any book that makes it to print is a labor of love and requires support from many different people. Many years ago, I told one of my junior high school teachers, Rita Farny, that one of my goals was to one day write and publish a book. Her belief that I could achieve my dreams inspired me, and many others, during those days at St. Boniface.

My loving wife, Jeanne, has been my life-long partner in chasing my dream of playing the PGA Tour and developing a career in business. It hasn't been a straight or easy path by any means. Her trust, counsel and support have been an irreplaceable part of any success I ever achieved, including writing this book.

My son, Ryan, and daughter, Taryn, endured many years of my travels, first for my golf career and then for my various business endeavors. We missed a great deal of time we might have spent together for which I am often saddened. That being said, we have also had countless wonderful times together and beautiful memories we share. I am very proud of the adults they have become and look forward to more time together in the future.

Special thanks go to my brother Roger, mentioned in the Preface, and his wife, PGA Professional Heidi Wright-Tennyson. Roger and I learned about golf together and pushed each other along the way. He has been a great brother, business partner and friend throughout my life. At the earliest stages, Roger and Heidi provided a critical eye and the feedback I needed to mold this book into something that, hopefully, every golfer could relate to and apply for their own benefit and enjoyment of the game.

I'd like to acknowledge and thank my parents, friends and all of the coaches I've had throughout my life in a variety of sports. They have been an important part of my journey, and I learned something from all of them along the way.

Finally, I want to acknowledge and thank the staff, members and my many friends at The Amelia Island Club and the Long Point golf course on Amelia Island in northeast Florida. Jeanne and I discovered this amazing place in 2013 and we have made it our home ever since. It gets better every year, and we look forward to spending many more years enjoying it.